tia

DORA the EXPLORER™
The Essential Guide

Written by Brian J. Bromberg

Señor Tucán

Tico

Baseball Star

Big Red Chicken

Baby Jaguar

Grumpy Old Troll

Benny

Funny Star

Isa

Tool Star

Swiper

Who is your favourite explorer?

NICK JR

DORA the EXPLORER™

Diego

Stars! ¡Las estrellas!

DK

Rocket Star

Boots

Dora

Azul the train

Map and Backpack

The Fiesta Trio

Contents

Contents

Let's Go!

Swing into an adventure with Dora the Explorer! Dora and her best friend Boots need your help to solve problems, save friends and outsmart that sneaky fox Swiper. Come on! ¡Vámonos!

Around the world

Dora and Boots need your help to explore forests, mountains and even outer space! Are you ready to go?

Everybody explore!

Each day brings a new and exciting adventure for Dora. But she couldn't do it without your help!

Dora never leaves home without Backpack and Map!

These boots are made for exploring, which is why Boots always wears them.

We can do it!

Dora must overcome many obstacles on her journey, whether it is in the rainforest or on top of a tall mountain.

Watch out for Swiper along the way!

Friends helping friends

Isa, Tico and Benny are good friends. They help Dora whenever they can, and they also count on her for help!

Spanish! ¡Español!

Dora speaks both English and Spanish. Learn to say it two ways with her!

You can lead the way!

Dora is not afraid to ask for help. She will often ask you to help her follow directions, count, sing or catch stars. Will you help her?

To cross the Muddy Mud, Dora needs the path with eight logs. Which is the path with eight logs?

Dora the Explorer

Dora is a helpful seven-year-old explorer who is always eager for her next adventure. She loves to explore with her best friend Boots, Backpack, Map and, of course, you!

Dora keeps everything that she needs in Backpack!

Dora always wears her bracelet on her right wrist.

How it all began

Dora met her best friend Boots, as well as Isa, Benny and Tico, on her very first adventure. They helped Dora find the Fiesta Trio's musical instruments and stopped Swiper from swiping Boots's boots!

Explorers need comfortable shoes! ¡Los zapatos!

Big sister

Dora is a fantastic big sister. She loves to help take care of her baby twin brother and sister. She likes to tell them stories about how they help her explore!

"Come on! ¡Vámonos!"

Dora adores

Dora loves to explore. Do you know what else she loves?

⭐ Dora loves her teddy bear, Osito.

⭐ She loves catching stars like her Abuela.

⭐ She loves taking care of her puppy, Perrito.

Football! ¡Fútbol!

Football is Dora's favourite sport. She enjoys playing with her friends on their team, the Golden Explorers! What is your favourite sport to play?

Dora's house!
¡La casa de Dora!

Home sweet home

Dora lives with her Mami, Papi, brother and sister in a beautiful yellow house. Both Abuela, Dora's grandmother, and her cousin Diego live nearby.

Boots

Boots is a furry, funny five-and-a-half-year-old monkey and Dora's closest friend. Boots only speaks English but Dora helps him learn Spanish words. Boots loves his red boots and exploring with Dora.

Monkey business

Boots hides in trees, does triple backflips and performs his Monkey Dance to make Dora laugh. This little monkey loves to be silly!

Boots can use his tail to swing from trees.

Going bananas!

One of Boots's favourite activities is to go exploring with Dora. Here are some other things that get him swinging in the trees.

★ He loves to snuggle with his cuddly stuffed dinosaur at bedtime.

★ Boots loves playing baseball.

★ Call Boots "Mr Riddles" because he loves to solve silly puzzles.

How many hairs does Boots have sticking up? 1,2,3! ¡Uno, dos, tres!

Favourite adventure

Boots's favourite thing in the world is visiting his daddy at work. Boots's daddy builds things like theme parks and this roller coaster!

Boots's fire truck

Boots loves playing with trucks, especially his super-duper toy fire truck with its loud siren. It looks just like Rojo the fire truck. What is your favourite toy?

Boots sings a song about his red boots called, "I Love My Boots".

Backpack

Backpack is Dora's trusty friend who travels everywhere with her, holding anything that she might need for her trip. Just like Dora, Backpack can speak both English and Spanish.

"Anything that you may need, I've got inside for you!"

This present talks!

Mami and Papi gave Backpack to Dora as a gift. But Backpack is more than a present: she's a great friend.

The Star Pocket

When Dora catches stars, they go into the Star Pocket that Backpack wears on her side.

Broken strap

Backpack always helps Dora, but sometimes Backpack needs help too. Once, she needed Dora to fix her strap with sticky tape!

Packed up

Helping Dora always makes Backpack smile!

Backpack holds a lot of things, so Dora usually needs your help to find just what she needs. Do you see the camera? ¡La cámara!

"Yum, yum, yum! ¡Delicioso!"

Here are some useful items that Backpack has carried for Dora.

★ ¡La corneta! The horn for their musical concert.

★ ¡Los binoculares! The binoculars to see far away.

★ ¡La llave! The key to open the locked gate.

★ ¡Los libros! The books to return to the library.

Map

If there's a place you've got to go, who's the one you need to know? The Map! He is Dora's funny, bouncy, helpful friend.

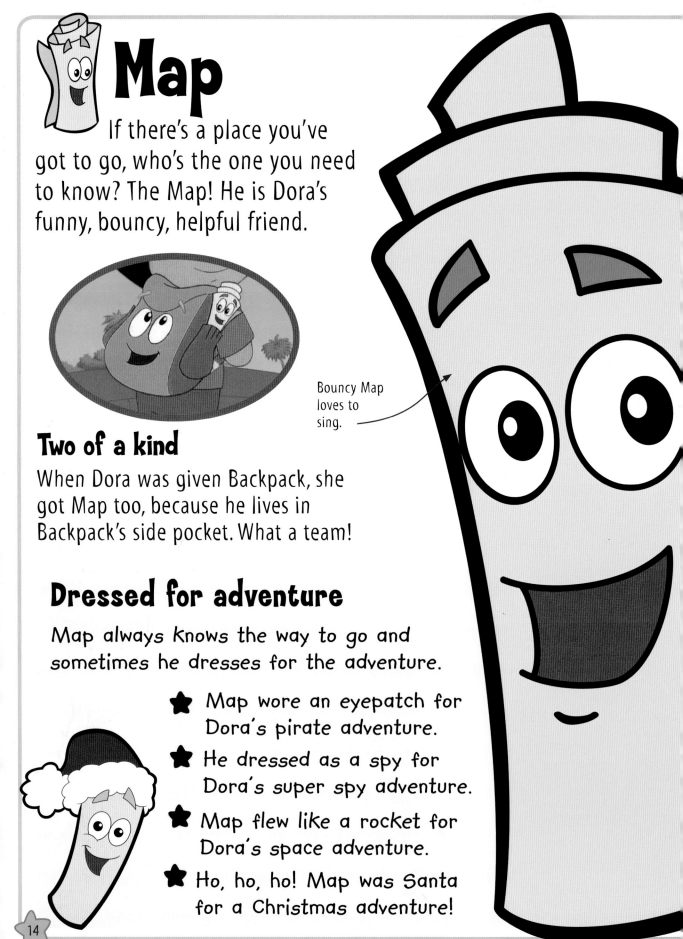

Bouncy Map loves to sing.

Two of a kind

When Dora was given Backpack, she got Map too, because he lives in Backpack's side pocket. What a team!

Dressed for adventure

Map always knows the way to go and sometimes he dresses for the adventure.

★ Map wore an eyepatch for Dora's pirate adventure.

★ He dressed as a spy for Dora's super spy adventure.

★ Map flew like a rocket for Dora's space adventure.

★ Ho, ho, ho! Map was Santa for a Christmas adventure!

A great guide

Map shows Dora where to go and tells her to watch out for Swiper!

Lost Map!

Dora needed to rescue Map when a Silly Bird thought Map was a stick. The bird used Map as part of a nest on Tallest Mountain!

Super Map!

A magic cape helped Map become a superhero! He flew up high in the air to give directions to Dora and used his superpowers to help her get home.

Star Catching

Stars! ¡Las estrellas! When Dora's Abuela gave her a Star Pocket, Dora became a Star Catcher, searching for giggly star friends. Sometimes, Dora catches Explorer Stars, too, who help her on her adventures.

Tool Star

Need something fixed? Tool Star is the Explorer Star with all the super-cool tools.

Tools, such as hammers, pop out of Tool St...

To Star Mountain!

When Swiper tossed Dora's necklace to the top of Star Mountain, Dora met many Explorer Stars who helped her to get it back!

Saltador

If Dora and Boots have to jump over something really tall, then they need Saltador, the super-jumping Explorer Star!

Glowy

Glowy is the bright-light Explorer Star. She can light up a tunnel for Dora or use her heat to melt ice.

Rocket Star

Blast off with Rocket Star, the fastest Explorer Star, who helps Dora to fly!

Woo Hoo

Meet more Explorer Stars

★ Woo Hoo is the peek-a-boo Explorer Star.

★ Artista is the colourful skywriting Explorer Star.

Artista

★ Mágico is full of magic and tricks.

★ Funny Star is really silly and pulls funny faces.

★ Noisy Star is the noisiest of the Explorer Stars.

★ Helada is the icy Explorer Star who can make snow.

★ Sliparonee is slippery and slides everywhere!

★ Disco Star has all the tunes for a great party.

★ Hero Star is the strongest of the Explorer Stars.

Swiper

"Oh, mannn!"

Swiper is a quick, sneaky fox who is always trying to swipe and hide Dora's stuff. He lives on Blueberry Hill, but he can pop up anywhere on his never-ending swiping missions. Watch out!

A blue mask disguises the sneaky fox.

Gloves! ¡Los guantes!

Master of disguise

Sometimes, Swiper tries to trick Dora by disguising himself as a tree, a cactus, a giant egg or even a polar bear. Dora and her friends have to watch out for the crafty fox.

"Swiper, no swiping!"

Help Dora and Boots stop Swiper by saying "Swiper, no swiping!" three times. Swiper will snap his fingers, say "Oh, mannn", and scamper off. But he will try again later!

Swiper's softer side

Swiper can sometimes be a nice fox, like when he decided to give back the present for Santa that he had swiped.

Swiper has a big, bushy tail.

Swiper's gadgets

Swiper uses many wild inventions to help him swipe, including a Robot Butterfly, a Super Swiping Machine and a SwiperCopter!

¡La Familia!

Papi loves to help Dora make delicious treats in the kitchen.

Dora lives with her Mami, Papi, twin brother and sister, and her puppy, Perrito. Dora's Abuela and her cousins, aunt, and uncle often visit. It is always busy at Dora's house!

Mami loves banana chocolate nut cake!

Mami and Papi

Mami is an explorer too because she's an archaeologist. Papi likes to hear all about Dora's many adventures. Mami and Papi gave Dora an Explorer's Kit to help her start exploring! Do you see the binoculars?

Family time

At dinner, Dora gathers with her parents, Abuela, her cousins and sometimes her friends too. They tell stories and spend time together.

Dora lives near to her Abuela — but visiting her grandmother is always an adventure!

A growing family

Before Dora became a big sister, just three people lived in her house. Then the twins were born. How many people live in Dora's house now? Five! ¡Cinco!

Abuela

Dora and her grandmother are very close. Sometimes, Abuela sends Dora on adventures. Once, she asked Dora to find her old friend Chocolate Tree.

Dora loves to hug Abuela.

Diego

Dora's cousin is an eight-year-old Animal Rescuer who rescues rainforest animal friends that are in trouble. He often swoops in to help Dora on her adventures too.

To the rescue!

Diego speaks English and Spanish, but he can also speak to animals with growls, squawks and hisses! That's why he's a great Animal Rescuer!

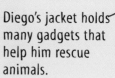

Diego's jacket holds many gadgets that help him rescue animals.

Animal Rescue Center

Dora and Boots love to visit Diego at the Animal Rescue Center where he works, deep in the rainforest. Diego helps his parents care for all kinds of animals.

Baby Jaguar

Playful Baby Jaguar is one of Diego's best animal friends. He just loves to go exploring with Diego and Dora – whether in the rainforest or on a pirate ship!

How many spots do you count on Baby Jaguar's head? (Answer on page 48)

Diego's Field Journal

Diego finds out everything that he needs to know about animals in his computerized Field Journal.

Diego's Field Journal holds information about animals.

Diego's family

Dora and Diego are close cousins. Diego loves to visit Dora's house with his mami and papi for parties.

Go, Diego, Go!

Dora has incredible animal adventures with Diego.

★ They saved Baby Jaguar when he was stuck near a waterfall.

★ They helped Boots when a gust of wind blew him away!

★ They took a dinosaur back to Dino Island.

Benny

Benny is a big, strong bull with a huge appetite and an even bigger heart. He often helps his friend Dora on her adventures, but it is usually Benny that is in need of Dora's help!

Benny is always ready to lend Dora a hand — or a hoof!

Benny's Barn

Benny lives in a large, red barn with his grandmother. Dora often visits him there. Dora also sees Benny at school and at all her fiestas. Benny loves party food, especially cake and ice cream!

Benny always wears his favourite blue, polka-dotted bandana.

24

Benny the potato!

Benny really needed Dora's help when he found a magic wand and turned himself into a potato! So, Dora helped her friend find a young wizard to turn him back into a bull.

On the moooove!

Benny loves to fly high in the sky with his friends in his hot air balloon — as long as it doesn't have a leak that Dora needs to fix with sticky tape!

Benny helps out

Benny isn't always a friend in need. He's also a friend indeed. He has helped Dora in many ways.

★ He played on Dora's Golden Explorers football team and helped them beat the Dinosaur Team.

★ Benny took Dora and Boots in his go-kart to meet Dora's new little twin brother and sister.

★ His strength helped Dora's team win the Super Adventure Race.

Tico

Tico is a Spanish-speaking squirrel and Dora's fastest friend. He is quick to speed in and save the day, though he might also ask Dora for help – in Spanish, of course!

Nutty about nuts

Like any other squirrel, Tico simply loves nuts!

A speedy squirrel

Tico helps to speed Dora and Boots along on their adventures in cars, boats, trains and even in his bicycle-powered aeroplane!

Tico the hero

Tico's mother is a firefighter, and, like her, Tico is a hero too. Tico has helped Dora many times.

Tico always wears his striped waistcoat.

★ Tico drove Dora all the way to the top of Tall Mountain.

★ He helped Dora recover her treasure chest from pirates.

★ Dora and Tico built a staircase of stars together in Fairytale Land.

"¡Rápido, amigos!"

Family tree

Tico has a big family. He lives with his mother and his cousins in the Nutty Forest.

¡Mi amigo Tico!

Tico speaks Spanish, so remember to say "¡Hola!" when you see him. Do you have friends who speak Spanish too?

Tico loves to drive his little yellow car. ¡El carro amarillo!

Isa

Isa is a smart, thoughtful iguana who lives in the Flowery Garden. She loves to help her good friends Dora and Boots.

"I love my flowers!"

Flower power

Isa enjoys growing flowers. But once, when she wished for her sunflower to grow really big, she needed Dora's help to get down!

Full of surprises

Isa is quiet and can easily blend into the background, especially in forests and gardens. She is very good at playing hide and seek! Do you see Isa?

Isa's flowers

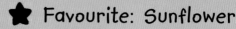

★ Favourite: Sunflower

★ Noisiest: Whistling Flower

★ Grooviest: Dancing Flower

★ Stickiest: Bug Trapper

Isa has beautiful, long eyelashes.

Hearts for friends

Isa loves all her friends but she especially likes to spend time with a certain monkey!

Isa's Flowery Garden

Isa has lots of exotic flowers in her Flowery Garden, and a few other surprises too — like her very own rocket ship!

Isa uses her tail to catch stars with Dora.

Fiesta Trio

Here comes the Fiesta Trio — a drum-playing frog, an accordion-playing grasshopper and a cymbal-playing snail. When Dora and Boots overcome an obstacle, the Fiesta Trio rewards them with a song.

How they met Dora

While riding to a concert for the Queen Bee, the Fiesta Trio lost their instruments. Dora saved the day by returning them to the silly trio!

Hear ye, hear ye!

If there is an important announcement to be made, the Fiesta Trio is the team to do it!

The grasshopper plays tunes on his accordion. ¡El acordeón!

The frog likes to bang the drum! ¡El tambor!

¡Instrumentos musicales!

Dora enjoys playing and listening to other musical instruments too.

★ ¡Las maracas!
   Shake the maracas!

★ ¡La guitarra!
   Strum the guitar!

★ ¡La corneta!
   Blow the horn!

Dora's flute

Boots knows that Dora loves music, so he gave her a flute as a Christmas present.

Silly concerts

There's no telling where the Fiesta Trio will pop up to play their music! They will ride by on a surfboard at the beach or pop out of a flower in a garden!

The snail likes to crash the cymbals!
¡Los címbalos!

Singing with Map

The Fiesta Trio sings along with Map when he shows Dora the way to go — they just can't resist a song!

Grumpy Old Troll

The Grumpy Old Troll is a cranky old soul who lives under Troll Bridge. He never lets anyone pass without solving one of his tricky riddles!

Troll Bridge

The Grumpy Old Troll must allow Dora and Boots to cross Troll Bridge when they solve his riddles. That is why Dora needs your help!

No rest for the Troll

Even when everyone else is sleeping, the Grumpy Old Troll stays awake to stump explorers with a riddle.

A tough riddle

Dora and Boots needed to make the Grumpy Old Troll laugh so that they could cross the bridge. Pulling silly faces did the trick!

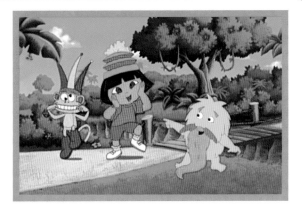

The Not-So-Grumpy Old Troll

The Grumpy Old Troll isn't always grumpy. Silly faces, parties, fireworks and purple flowers make him do his happy dance!

The Grumpy Old Troll's Riddles

★ 1. Here is one of my toughest quizzers. To cut through the net, you'd need a pair of _____

a. Scissors   b. Socks   c. Maracas

★ 2. Solving this riddle will make you proud. Find the thing that makes a noise that's loud.

a. A horn

b. A book

c. Candy

The Grumpy Old Troll's long beard drags on the ground.

Answers on page 48

35

A Helping Hand

Every fiesta needs a cak ¡Un pastel!

It's Dora the Explorer to the rescue! Dora and Boots are always ready to help their very good friends, big or small.

Big Red Chicken

Dora and Boots saved Big Red Chicken's Super Silly Fiesta by helping him find his cake. It was on top of his head!

"Bawk Thank you for finding my cake!"

Big Red Chicken is dressed nicely for his Super Silly Fiesta!

Big blue laces

Dora has helped the Big Red Chicken many times. When he couldn't tie his shoes, Dora save the day!

Señor Tucán

When Señor Tucán needs super spies for a mission, he knows who to call – Dora and Boots. In return, he'll fly by to help Dora whenever he can.

Señor Tucán speaks Spanish!

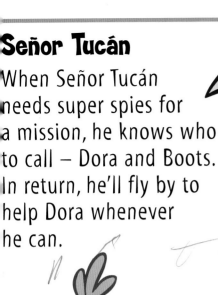

Baby Blue Bird

Dora and Boots helped Baby Blue Bird find her way back to her Mami in the Little Blue Tree.

Señor Tucán's multicoloured feathers help him to hide in the colourful rainforest.

Thanks for the help! ¡Gracias!

Here are a few friends who want to say thank you to Dora for helping them to...

★ "... catch a wish so I could wish myself home!" – the Wizzle

★ "... win a whistle at Big Yellow Station!" – Azul the train

★ "... become a real circus lion!" – León the Lion

★ "... return to Coquí Island and get my voice back!" – El Coquí

★ "... return to my family on Crab Island!" – Baby Crab

★ "... save a kitten who was caught in a tree!" – Rojo the fire truck

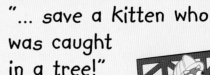

Dora's Adventures

With your help, Dora has explored some amazing places, including Rainbow Rock, the North Pole and Red Rock. Which place did you like the best?

Rainbow Rock

On Best Friend's Day, Dora and Boots needed your help to meet up at Rainbow Rock. When they got there, they ate yummy strawberries!

There's Swiper! "Swiper, no swiping!"

A gift for Santa

At Christmas, Dora wanted to give a gift to Santa. Dora and Boots put on their warm clothes and went all the way to the North Pole!

Fish out of water

Dora and Boots travelled in a submarine to take a Baby Red Fish home to Red Rock, far out in the middle of the ocean.

Dora's destinations

Dora is an explorer on the go! Her journeys have also taken her to:

★ Star Mountain

★ the Desert

★ Nursery Rhyme Land

★ Outer Space

★ around the whole world!

Star Mountain has a star at the very top.

Pirate Adventure

It is high adventure on the high seas when Dora and friends set sail on an epic, musical journey to get their treasure chest back from the Pirate Piggies!

"Yo ho ho!"

Shiver me timbers!

Dora and her friends are putting on a Pirate Play when the Pirate Piggies take Dora's treasure chest of costumes to Treasure Island. They think the chest is full of gold!

Treasure Map

Map tells Dora that they need to sail over the Seven Seas, under the Singing Bridge and on to Treasure Island to get the treasure back. Say it with Map: "Seas, Bridge, Treasure Island!"

1234567

Anchors aweigh!

As they go through the seas and under the bridge, the pirate pals have lots to do.

⭐ Diego saves Baby Jaguar in the sea.

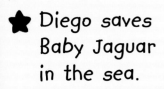

Say to the cannon, "Give us back our treasure!"

Pirate Parrot is a salty old sea bird.

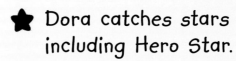

⭐ Dora catches stars including Hero Star.

⭐ The friends go through the Foggy Fog.

⭐ Isa steers around the Big Bad Rocks.

⭐ Dora fixes the pirate ship's steering wheel!

It's a treasure chest full of costumes.

Seafaring Swiper

At Treasure Island, Dora must stop Swiper from swiping the chest. "Swiper, no swiping!"

Ahoy, Pirate Piggies!

When the Pirate Piggies see that there are costumes and not gold inside the treasure chest, they apologize for their mistake. They love to sing so they join in with Dora's Pirate Play!

Showtime!

Dressed in their pirate hats, hooks and boots, the friends perform their pirate play for their families. They couldn't have done it without you!

The Purple Planet

It is an out-of-this-world adventure when Dora and Boots blast into outer space. They need to take home five lost space creatures whose flying saucer has landed on Earth. It's a long way to the Purple Planet.

The Purple Planet! ¡El planeta morado!

Dora's wears her space suit on the Purple Planet.

New friends

Dora meets the cute space creatures named Flinky, Inky, Plinky, Dinky and Al who need help getting home.

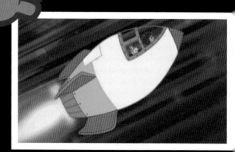

Isa's rocket ship

The space creatures' flying saucer broke on Earth, so Dora and Boots borrow Isa's rocket ship to fly them home!

Star Map

Map knows the way, even in outer space! He tells Dora to travel through the Milky Way, past the Space Rocks and on to the Purple Planet!

Teddy to the rescue

Dora can see a teddy bear constellation, showing her the direction she should take to get through the Milky Way!

Homeward bound

Dora and Boots land on the Purple Planet. Flinky, Inky, Plinky, Dinky and Al are finally home. Hooray!

Flinky

Inky

Plinky

Dinky

Al

Fairytale Land

Dora and Boots are exploring Fairytale Land when the Mean Witch turns Boots into Sleeping Boots! Dora needs your help to become la Princesa Dora and save her friend!

"Zzzzzz...."

Boots is under the witch's spell.

Welcome to Fairytale Land

Dora and Boots pass through a magical gate to Fairytale Land. This is an enchanted place of castles, lollipops and fairytale friends like the Gingerbread Man and Snow White!

The Mean Witch

The Mean Witch disguises herself as a tree and hands Boots a banana that sends him into a deep sleep. Only Dora can break the spell.

Princess power!

To become a true princess and wake Sleeping Boots, Dora must:

⭐ find the Dragon's Red Ring.

⭐ teach the Giant Rocks to sing.

⭐ turn winter into spring.

⭐ bring the Moon to the Queen and King.

Dragon's cave

Finding the Dragon's Red Ring breaks the Witch's spell over him. Dora finds out that the Dragon is really a prince!

The Bag of Sunshine will melt the winter snow.

The Giant Giant

Dora teaches the Giant Rocks to sing and finds the Giant's Puppy. The Giant Giant gives Dora a Bag of Sunshine to turn winter into spring.

La Princesa Dora wears a shiny dress.

High in the sky

Dora and her friends build a star-staircase up into the sky so that they can bring the Moon to the Queen and King. Dora is almost a princess!

A true princess

The King turns Dora into a true princess. On a unicorn, la Princesa Dora rides back to Boots and wakes him up with a big hug!

Dance to the Rescue

When a sly Dancing Elf traps Swiper in a bottle, dancing Dora needs to win One Big Wish at the Royal Dance Contest to save Swiper!

Swiper let the Dancing Elf out of the bottle, so Swiper had to go in!

The Dancing Elf

The Dancing Elf tries to stop Dora from winning One Big Wish so he doesn't have to go back in the bottle!

Which way, Map?

To get to the King's Dance Contest, Dora needs to go through the Pyramid, across the Ocean and to the Castle!

In the pyramid

Tico flies Dora and Boots to the pyramid. There they:

★ march like ants!

★ wiggle like spiders!

★ slither and slide like snakes!

On the ocean wave

Isa helps Dora and Boots get to the sea and the Pirate Piggies help them cross the ocean.

The King's Castle

Dora and Boots need fancy clothes so that they can enter King Juan el Bobo's Castle. Benny comes to the rescue with a bow tie for Boots and a pretty dress for Dora.

A royal dance

At the contest, Dora does the Ants in your Pants dance and dances like a fish. She even gets the King's mummy on her feet!

A flower in the hair is a pretty finishing touch to Dora's fancy dress.

Everyone can dance!

Dora wins One Big Wish and frees Swiper. She asks the King to let the Dancing Elf stay outside the bottle. Then, everyone can dance together. Let's celebrate by doing a dance! ¡Baila!

Fancy footwork!

We Did It!

When Dora and Boots complete an adventure, they always celebrate by singing "We Did It"! Dora and Boots love singing and dancing with other explorers – like you!

"We did it! ¡Lo hicimos!"

Let's celebrate!

It's always good to celebrate with family and friends! Who is celebrating with Dora here?

Every party needs music. Hooray for the Fiesta Trio!

Fiesta time

Dora's friends have helped her explore so they join the fiesta! How many of Dora's amigos do you count here?

A piñata is filled with sweet treats.

Sometimes Dora even invites Swiper to the party!

Favourite adventures

Dora has gone on many adventures. At the end of each adventure, Dora asks you what your favourite part of the trip was.

★ Dora loved the adventure when she discovered that she was a big sister!

★ Boots loved his special day when he visited his daddy at work!

Boots loves to monkey around.

★ Which adventure did you love best? What was your favourite part?

Answers

Page 23

There are 10 spots on Baby Jaguar's face

Page 33

1. a (Scissors)

2. a (A horn)

LONDON, NEW YORK, MUNICH,
MELBOURNE, AND DELHI

Senior Art Editor Guy Harvey
Project Editor Laura Gilbert
Publishing Manager Simon Beecroft
Brand Manager Robert Perry
Category Publisher Alex Allan
DTP Designer Lauren Egan
Production Rochelle Talary

First Published in Great Britain in 2006 by
Dorling Kindersley Limited
80 Strand, London WC2R 0RL
A Penguin Company
06 07 08 09 10 10 9 8 7 6 5 4 3 2 1

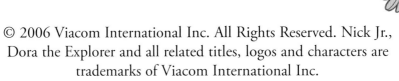

A CIP catalogue record for this book is available from the British Library.

ISBN-13 978-1-40531-426-8   ISBN-10 1-4053-1426-5

Colour reproduction by Media Development and Printing Ltd, UK
Printed and bound in China by Hung Hing Offset Printing Company Ltd.

www.nickjr.co.uk

www.nickelodeon.com.au

ACKNOWLEDGEMENTS
DK Publishing would like to thank:
Kate Serafini at Nickelodeon for all her help.

Discover more at
www.dk.com